PRANKSTERS VS. AUTOCRATS

T0339369

Mccourtney Institute for Democracy

The Pennsylvania State University's McCourtney Institute for Democracy (http://democracyinstitute.la.psu.edu) was founded in 2012 as an interdisciplinary center for research, teaching, and outreach on democracy. The institute coordinates innovative programs and projects in collaboration with the Center for American Political Responsiveness and the Center for Democratic Deliberation.

Laurence and Lynne Brown Democracy Medal

The Laurence and Lynne Brown Democracy Medal recognizes outstanding individuals, groups, and organizations that produce exceptional innovations to further democracy in the United States or around the world. In even numbered years, the medal spotlights practical innovations, such as new institutions, laws, technologies, or movements that advance the cause of democracy. Awards given in odd numbered years highlight advances in democratic theory that enrich philosophical conceptions of democracy or empirical models of democratic behavior, institutions, or systems.

PRANKSTERS VS. AUTOCRATS

WHY DILEMMA ACTIONS ADVANCE NONVIOLENT ACTIVISM

SRDJA POPOVIC
WITH
SOPHIA A. McCLENNEN

CORNELL SELECTS

an imprint of

CORNELL UNIVERSITY PRESS

Ithaca and London

Cornell Selects, *an imprint of Cornell University Press, provides a forum for advancing provocative ideas and fresh viewpoints through outstanding digital and print publications. Longer than an article and shorter than a book, titles published under this imprint explore a diverse range of topics in a clear and concise format—one designed to appeal to any reader. Cornell Selects publications continue the press's long tradition of supporting high quality scholarship and sharing it with the wider community, promoting a culture of broad inquiry that is a vital aspect of the mission of Cornell University.*

Open access edition funded by the McCourtney Institute for Democracy at Pennsylvania State University

First published 2020 by Cornell University Press

Library of Congress Cataloging-in-Publication Data
Library of Congress Control Number: 2020941265

Contents

PRANKSTERS VS. AUTOCRATS

Introduction

I've spent the last fifteen years heading the Centre for Applied Nonviolent Action and Strategy (CANVAS), an NGO that assists prodemocracy activists in Asia, Africa, Latin America, the Middle East, and also parts of the former Soviet Union.[1] For over two decades I have been an advocate for democracy and human rights. Since my freshman year at Belgrade University, as I have led struggles for democracy, I've been under surveillance, arrested, even beaten up. I've also traveled the world to train prodemocracy activists, written books, lectured internationally, and taught students on the topic.

I used to think I'd become famous for my music, not for activism. When I was just twenty, I released my first album with the goth rock band BAAL. I played bass guitar and I was pretty good. We had a following. But then it became too hard to ignore what was happening in my country. The next thing I knew I was part of a student-led group that effectively took down Slobodan Milošević. Well, actually, that's not exactly right. We didn't just accidentally overthrow a dictator. We used unique and specific tactics. Over the years, as I've worked with activists across the globe, I've refined my approach to the most effective techniques for overthrowing autocrats.

I've had many thrilling experiences helping nonviolent shakers and shapers push for positive social change. In this process of turning my personal experiences into strategies and tactics I can teach others, I have come to realize that successful nonviolent movements tend to share a common ingredient: they use *dilemma actions* that force those in power into a lose-lose situation. In other words, if you can trap those in power in an irresolvable dilemma, the action is more likely to accomplish its goals. Those goals might include recruiting more supporters, spreading the movement's vision, attracting attention to the cause, pressuring unjust leaders to cede power, or advancing democracy. I realized that if I could explain how, why, and to what extent dilemma actions succeed in advancing democracy, I could help activist groups become far more effective—regardless of whether they were planning their next move in a café in Cairo or in a home office in New York City.

But before I explain all my goals for this project, let's take a moment and play one of my favorite games. It's called "Pretend Police." It's fun. Here goes. Pretend you're the police in

Ankara, Turkey. A few days ago, a couple of security guards in one of the busiest subway stations in town spotted a couple making out on the platform. Being strict Muslims, the guards were annoyed by such immodest behavior in public, so they did the only thing they could really do, which was get on the subway's PA system and ask all passengers to behave themselves and stop kissing each other. Because everyone in Ankara has smartphones, the incident reached the press within minutes; by the afternoon, politicians opposed to the ruling Islamist-based party realized that they had a golden egg in their hands. They encouraged their supporters to stage huge demonstrations to protest this silly anti-smooching bias.

This is where you come in. On Saturday, the day of the demonstration, you show up in uniform, baton at hand, ready to keep the peace. Walking into the subway station, you see more than a hundred young men and women chanting antigovernment slogans and provoking your colleagues. Someone shoves someone. Someone loses their cool. Soon it's a full-blown riot.

If you're seriously playing along, it's probably not hard to figure out what to do. You're a police officer, and you've probably spent a whole week at the academy training for situations just like this. It's what police all over the world do. You put on your riot gear, you move in, you get in formation, and you start to thump your baton on your shield to intimidate the crowd. You probably don't feel too bad about it, either.

3

You're only doing your job, protecting yourself and your fellow cops. It takes you an hour, maybe two, before thirty or forty of the protesters are in jail, ten or twenty are in the hospital, and the rest have run away. You return to the precinct house, drink a coffee with your buddies, and go to bed feeling content with a day's work.

That was easy. Now, let's play again.

It's Saturday morning. You arrive at the subway station. There are more than a hundred people there, protesting against the censorious announcement from the day before. But they're not saying anything against the government. They're not shouting or chanting. They're kissing each other loudly, making those gross slurpy sounds nobody likes, drooling and giggling. There are almost no signs to be seen, but the ones you do notice have little pink hearts on them and read "Kiss Me" or "Free Hugs." The women are in short-sleeved, low-cut blouses. The men have their button-downs on. No one seems to notice you—they're too busy holding each other's heads as they suck face.

Now what? Go ahead and game it out if you'd like, but let me save you the trouble. The answer is that there's nothing you can do. It's not only that the amorous demonstrators aren't breaking any laws; it's also that their attitude makes a world of difference. If you're a cop, you spend a lot of time thinking about how to deal with people who are violent. But nothing in your training prepares you for dealing with people who are funny and peaceful.

4

The story I have just told you really did happen in Turkey in May 2013. And it is an example of what we might call an *accidental* dilemma action. It was a protest that worked because the protesters instinctively understood that it would be effective. They lucked out. But what would have happened if they had thought through their tactic as part of a well-understood strategy? What if the kissing—and putting the police force in an irresolvable dilemma—had been planned from the start? Moreover, how can we ensure this kind of success for other nonviolent activists who want to strengthen democracy?

Turning Luck into a Strategy

Examples of accidental dilemma actions abound. Most smart activists know that if they can find a peaceful, creative way to put an authority in a tight spot, they will help their cause. But what would happen if we took these accidents and made them deliberate, well-constructed strategies tailored for a specific context? It might help even more.

Activists who have implemented dilemma actions know that success requires paying attention to several critical elements. You have to know how the repressive power works, and you have to know what will win the public over. Public outcry supporting your movement is critical.

This is what makes a dilemma action different from your average nonviolent protest—and generally more successful than other forms of nonviolent resistance. Not all types of nonviolent resistance force a response; if the authorities can ignore you, you haven't created a dilemma action. So, depending on the level of restrictions in your country and the number of people you draw to your vigil, rally, or march, you might put a lot of effort into something that the authorities can just blow off. Other times the authorities will shut your protest down, but no one will care. That happens when you haven't won over the public. Worst of all, a protest not crafted with public opinion in mind can backfire for the movement—leaving the public angry and irritated at the protesters. So, if you block a road in the middle of rush hour and keep a lot of average folks from getting to work, and then you get removed by the police, the public may actually be on the police's side.

This is what makes a dilemma action different from your average nonviolent protest. Our 2007 CANVAS Core Curriculum states, "Dilemma actions are designed to create a 'response dilemma' or 'lose-lose' situation for public authorities by forcing them to either concede some public space to protesters or make themselves look absurd or heavy-handed by acting against the protest."[2] Dilemma actions—as part of a structured, strategic direct action—are a valuable component of effective nonviolent struggle. And humorous ones, or laughtivism, in particular, can be even more successful in advancing particular goals than nonviolent resistance in general. This route offers you great opportunities for success.

I have spent a lot of time learning about dilemma actions worldwide through my work at CANVAS, the organization we founded after our Serbian movement's success went global. With colleagues, I have spent over fifteen years training and consulting with democracy and human rights defenders from across the globe. And yes, very often part of this training process is focused on how to implement creative tactics that include a dilemma element and a dose of humor for the direct action my fellow activists are planning to perform.

Receiving a Brown Medal for Democracy moved this passion to a new gear. In January 2020, I teamed up with my colleague and friend, Sophia McClennen, a global expert on political satire. We assembled a team of researchers to put dilemma actions under a microscope and test our concept within a more rigorous, data-based, academic foundation.[3] My personal experience had shown me that, as a tool, dilemma actions can and do make a difference for democracy, but what would happen, we wondered, if we could prove it? This essay attempts an answer, and in the process, you'll read about the origins, nature, background, use, and effects of dilemma actions. We pull results from analyzing forty-four case studies of a century's worth of dilemma actions. We selected such a geographically and temporally wide series of examples so that we could analyze how dilemma actions work across diverse historical and cultural contexts. As you read this, we'll explain why and how dilemma actions work. And you'll learn how to think like an effective organizer. If you already are an organizer, you'll learn how to design actions that are fun, funny, and effective.

A Dilemma for Every Aspiring Autocrat

Our research, as well as the world arena in which the struggle for democracy takes place, is not limited to autocracies. It is no small paradox that Western democracies long considered at "low risk" for an erosion of democratic institutions now require new and vigorous protection. We have seemed to forget President's Reagan words, "Freedom is a fragile thing and is never more than one generation away from extinction."[4] Of course, pushing a warmongering autocrat out of power is different from defending established democracies that have recently come under threat. But the risks for democracy remain real and global. We are currently witnessing democratic backsliding in countries that are relative newcomers to the European Union, including Poland and Hungary, which joined the EU in 2004. Human rights are also threatened in established "traditional" democracies like France, the United States, and the United Kingdom as immigrants and refugees have been denied basic rights and protections. The rising tide of illiberalism, racism, and xenophobia is a grave concern from Cape Town and New Delhi to Paris and Minneapolis.

When seeking to end any dictatorship anywhere, the task is to erode the tools and institutions that serve the autocrat who abuses power. Indeed, the goal is to upend the status quo. *Defending* democracy, however, means finding ways to defend democratic institutions and principles from those who want to undermine them, even if they're elected officials. It means creating leverage to block governments or political forces that seek to dismantle the pillars of democracy—such as an independent judiciary, parliamentary oversight, minority rights, and a free press. This is why we'll look at many examples of dilemma actions coming from countries with developed democratic traditions and institutions, including Germany, Finland, Canada, Spain, and the United States.

Dilemma actions are an effective tool for a range of situations. They have been used to advance democracy, human rights, and accountability struggles across the globe. They break down fear and apathy and offer the public an energizing way to resist oppressive authority. They can shift public narratives of mighty opponents from "scary and powerful" to "weak and laughable." They also work as a recruiting tool for new members because they show the public that engaging in nonviolent resistance can be fun and satisfying. They lead to media coverage and social media awareness because these tactics make for entertaining stories—authoritarians look foolish and the protesters look creative, cool, and unafraid. Dilemma actions succeed: they often lead to social change and advances in democracy. And, even more important, groups that engage in dilemma actions inspire others, leading to replication of their tactics, adjusted for different contexts and types of struggles.

But to what extent? Are there examples of times when a group succeeded in only some of these outcomes? What happened when they failed? As we think about nonviolent ways to advocate for a future we want to live in, it helps to learn from the past. This essay's goal is to offer more specific accounts of model dilemma actions and to assess their success across a range of metrics. We know that some of you may be reading about dilemma actions for the first time, and we want you most of all to become familiar with the idea by reading a lot of clever examples and learning the basics of how they work. But if you are interested in having a deeper understanding of dilemma actions, whether to advance your activism or your understanding of nonviolent resistance, at the end we talk briefly about how some of these metrics support or impede one another. For instance, did some examples attract new supporters and media attention but fail in other ways? Did others succeed in ousting an autocrat but only at the expense of violent reprisals for the movement's leaders? Do dilemma actions that include elements of humor and irony—what we call *laughtivism*—have a higher success rate? Does laughing at dictators deflate their power?

We argue that dilemma actions, performed by nonviolent movements around the world in a wide variety of circumstances, are a valuable component of successful nonviolent struggle. They produce outsized benefits for the practitioners, catch their opponents off guard, and even trigger self-harming responses from opposing stakeholders. Furthermore, dilemma actions— especially when they include humor—can counteract fear and apathy, two underestimated enemies of reform. Fear and apathy drive the status quo and block positive social change in any society that hopes for a better future. But humor melts fear and earns goodwill, often adding a "cool factor" to activism that draws support.

A Brief History of
the Dilemma Action

Here's the foundational assumption of this essay: any resistance movement has a much greater chance at success if its leaders choose nonviolent action.

You may opt to engage in nonviolent resistance, following the teachings of Mohandas K. Gandhi or Martin Luther King Jr., on principle alone. But even if you aren't swayed by that, nonviolence is a better strategic choice because it works. So, if you don't choose it on principle, choose it for its success rate.

Many people assume that violence is the only way to overthrow a violent regime. There is clear proof, however, that nonviolence is a better political strategy for resistance groups. A study conducted by Erica Chenoweth and Maria J. Stephan found that nonviolent movements are twice as likely to succeed as violent movements.[5] Nonviolent protests have a success rate of 53 percent, in contrast with

23 percent success for protests with violence. They also showed that when we talk about winning converts over to a cause, the bar isn't really that high. They explain that if just 3.55 percent of the population participates in your movement, it guarantees political change. That's right. Movements with active support of only 3.55 percent of the population have never failed.[6] Also, Chenoweth and Stephan show clear evidence that it is easier to expand your ranks if your campaign is seen as representing a broad view. If you appear extremist or on the fringe, potential supporters are likely to shy away from you.

Even better, research also proves that it is a lot harder for authorities to use violence against a nonviolent action. As you saw in the kissing protest, when those involved are laughing and having fun, police belligerence isn't going to help the regime. It will look heavy-handed and send even more centrists flying into the arms of the resistance.

If these aren't enough reasons to choose nonviolence, there are more.

Dilemma actions are a key tool in nonviolent resistance because they have worked for decades. Gandhi, in fact, was an early practitioner. But while this sort of resistance has a long history, and while scholars have made efforts to theorize and describe it, no systematic, clear, and specific "strategic framework" for devising adaptable dilemma actions has existed until now. If protests are to work reliably, wherever people are repressed by undemocratic regimes, budding activists need to know how to effectively design them. A clear blueprint for developing a dilemma action will help activists assess their unique situations of repression so that they can put oppressive power in a lose-lose situation, one that attracts positive media attention and expands the membership of the nonviolent movement.

Dilemma actions, according to our experience and research and discussed in our "CANVAS Core Curriculum—Guide to Effective Nonviolent Struggle," ideally put the opponent in a situation where it must either (a) grant a nonviolent movement's demand, or (b) act in a way that sacrifices some of its own support and damages its public image.[7] Historically, dilemma actions have proved to expand the political space and given movements small victories that help them build momentum and a record of success. Part of that success stems from being rooted in popular, easy-to-agree-with beliefs (like the idea that young people should be allowed to kiss). Media attention follows, as does a swath of public opinion. This is why, for example, something like the national anthem protests by US National Football League players sparked such controversy and were unsuccessful. Initially, players nonviolently protested against police brutality and for African American rights; but as the media conversation shifted to whether the protest disrespected the national anthem (and by extension, the flag and military veterans' sacrifices), the initial, easy-to-agree-with issue became a different, controversial one. The public debated whether the national anthem should be uniformly respected at football games, instead of joining a protest over blatant racial disparities.

Activists who tap into broad public sentiment are more likely to precipitate a response from those in power than activists who seem fringe. If you can be marginalized, then those in power can ignore you. This is why, for example, when women leave their homes to march and bang pots, they get a lot of attention. These sorts of nonviolent protests are easy for others to join, even if they are not true dilemma actions that require a response.

Also, when the activists who are performing dilemma actions are individually popular and visible, the dilemma they present to their opponent is even greater. That is, high public regard protects you and makes you harder to ignore. This is one place where humor and playfulness really help. In the United States the Yes Men (Andy Bichlbaum and Mike Bonanno) impersonate businessmen to shame the actual businesses they are impersonating.[8] In one hilarious example, Bichlbaum impersonated a Dow Chemical spokesperson on BBC World on the twentieth anniversary of the Bhopal disaster.[9] Dressed in a suit and looking quite serious, he apologized for Dow's actions and stated that they planned to sell Union Carbide, the company responsible for the chemical disaster, and use the $12 billion in profits to pay for medical care, environmental remediation, and to fund research into the hazards of other Dow products. The whole thing was a hoax. But it worked. It drew massive mainstream attention to Dow's failed response to the disaster, and one reason it did so was that Bichlbaum was such an earnest and likable prankster.

The first well-documented example of an ingenious dilemma action was the Salt March campaign of 1930, launched by Gandhi during the Indian independence struggle against British colonial occupation. In short: making salt required only boiling seawater and collecting the salt residue, but the British passed laws granting themselves control of the production of salt, generating tax income for the colonial government.[10] When Gandhi organized mass defiance of the British salt law, the British government was faced with a dilemma about how to respond. If the British occupiers arrested Gandhi and other salt-law breakers, they would look ridiculous for being so repressive about something as simple and basic to everyone's life as salt. This would damage their legitimacy and make heroes out of the activists. However, if they did not take action against the salt-law breakers, they would not only lose the salt monopoly and tax revenues, they would also lose authority in the eyes of the millions of people that they were trying to rule. The British opted to arrest Gandhi, a move that made them look excessively repressive, and the rest is history.

Another well-known example of a dilemma action was the "Farmer's Hat" protest by the Burmese opposition during the darkest times of the military dictatorship and oppression. The bamboo farmer's hat was a traditional garment for hundreds of thousands of Burmese farmers. It also symbolized the National League for Democracy party, which was headed by the Nobel laureate Aung San Suu Kyi, during the campaign leading to the May 1990 elections. The nonviolent action of simply wearing a hat, which the regime had prohibited as "subversive," created a dilemma for the ruling military authority (commonly referred to as SLORC). If SLORC arrested people for wearing a common hat, it would lose additional credibility among the populace. But if SLORC did nothing and allowed people to wear the hat without punishment, then the population could openly flout the regime.[11] Given the extraordinarily repressive nature of SLORC, one might have expected them to immediately arrest the hat wearers, but instead, they delayed in reacting—a move that allowed the act of wearing these hats to become widespread. Their inability to deal with this low-risk dilemma action on a national level encouraged thousands of prodemocracy Burmese to wear these hats. These simple bamboo hats thus became a national symbol of the opposition for the next decade and helped build momentum for the resistance.

Other contemporary and widely reported dilemma actions come from struggles for racial equality. During the US civil rights movement, African Americans and their allies violated a ban that prevented black patrons from sitting and eating at the lunch counters of restaurants and department stores in Nashville, Tennessee (and elsewhere). This nonviolent direct action was designed not only to create a dilemma for local authorities and businesses, but also to overturn the myth that all white Americans supported racial segregation. During several sit-ins, lunch counters were disrupted and businesses lost money. Media coverage increased, as over a hundred black students and white supporters were arrested in the face of police intimidation and violence by citizens. Protest telegrams began to come in from across the country, including from celebrities such as singer Harry Belafonte and former first lady Eleanor Roosevelt. The mayor of Nashville was faced with a dilemma. Keeping the students off segregated lunch counters and putting them in jail by the hundreds would hurt the city's reputation and outrage business owners more than allowing them to continue breaking segregation laws. In the end, the movement won and the lunch counters became integrated, although American's broader fight for racial justice continues to this day.

Laughing Makes a Difference

Sometimes dilemma actions are spiced with an element of humor. In those cases, we are looking at a specific strategic application of a tactic we popularly call *laughtivism*. In Serbia in 1999, I and dozens of my friends founded the nonviolent youth movement, Otpor. We frequently and strategically used this specific form of dilemma action—laughtivism—to challenge and ridicule Serbian dictator

Slobodan Milošević and his unpopular wife, Mirjana Marković. Mocking and teasing created a dilemma for the police, who were faced with two unfavorable choices: (a) arrest harmless, popular young people who were making others laugh, along with a ton of pedestrians and random passersby who were enjoying their own participation in street theater; or (b) ignore the action, disobey an order to stop the "humiliation" of the dictator and his family, and thus encourage other groups and individuals to challenge the regime in a similar manner.

One of our most successful dilemma actions was called "Dime for Change." My fellow Otpor activists painted a picture of Slobodan Milošević's face onto a large petrol barrel in a downtown shopping area in the capital city of Belgrade. People were invited to throw a few "dimes for change" into the barrel and buy themselves a chance to hit the painted portrait of our dear president with a bat. Soon curious bystanders lined up for a swing. People started to stare, then to point, then to laugh. Before long some parents were encouraging their children who were too small for the bat to kick the barrel. Everybody was having fun, and the *clang* of the barrel echoed all the way down to Kalemegdan Park. It didn't take long for the president's portrait to get beaten beyond recognition.

As this was happening, my friends and I were sitting outside an adjacent café. It was fun to see all these people blowing off steam. But the best part, we knew, still lay ahead. Ten minutes later, a patrol car stopped nearby and two pudgy policemen stepped out. The Serbian police's first instinct, we knew, would be to arrest perpetrators and protesters. Ordinarily they'd arrest the demonstration's organizers, but we were anonymously spectating from a busy café. That left the officers with only two bad choices. They could arrest the people lining up to smack the barrel—including waiters from nearby cafés, people holding shopping bags, and a bunch of parents with children—or they could just arrest the barrel itself. If they went for the people, they would cause an outrage, as there's hardly a law on the books prohibiting violence against rusty metal cylinders, and mass arrests of innocent bystanders are the surest way for a regime to radicalize even its passive citizens.

The two rotund officers shooed away the onlookers, positioned themselves on either side of the filthy barrel, and hauled it off in their squad car. But of course, we had invited several photojournalists to our spectacle—the next day, our stunt ended up on the cover of two national newspapers, the type of publicity that you literally couldn't buy. That picture—two policemen dragging an old barrel with Milošević's face to the patrol car—was truly worth a thousand words. It told anyone who so much as glimpsed it that Milošević's feared police had been turned into a punchline.

We were so proud of our little prank. We naively thought that we, the Serbs, were the first to marry a dilemma action with an element of humor and mockery. We boldly even decided to give it a label, *laughtivism*. You can imagine how disappointed I was later, as I started doing more research on nonviolent protests, to find that our approach had already been invented decades ago.

Consider the Polish Solidarity movement. It was a cold February evening in 1982 when the people of Świdnik, a small town in eastern Poland, took their television sets for a walk. Tired of the nightly routine of watching smiley announcers with fancy haircuts reading government-approved scripts that were ridiculously rosy and full of lies, activists decided to protest by not watching the news. But for the boycott to work, it had to be both public and subtle enough to avoid a police crackdown. Like comics trying out new material, they improvised. At first, they made a point of unplugging their sets and placing them on their window-sills every evening at 7:30 p.m. It was a good first step, but it wasn't funny, and therefore it was uninspiring. So someone procured a bunch of wheelbarrows and encouraged their friends to take their TVs down to the street, load them up, and wheel them around town. Before too long, anyone walking the streets of Świdnik at dusk could see friends and neighbors ambling and laughing, pushing along wheel-barrows like baby carriages, holding TVs instead of babies, using the half-hour previously spent listening to the official newscast to greet one another, gossip, and share in the thrill of standing up to the regime together.

It was a great gag, and the practice soon spread to other Polish towns. Flabbergasted, the government weighed its options. It couldn't arrest anyone; there was no law specifying that Polish citizens couldn't push a TV down the street. All they could do was move the 10 p.m. curfew up to 7:00 p.m., thereby forcing everyone indoors and thus showing their powerlessness to contain criticism, a move that outraged the Polish public even more.

Dilemma Actions Today

While nonviolent action wasn't new in the twentieth century, there is no doubt that it began as a conscious political strategy in the twentieth century and that its use is on the rise in the twenty-first.[12] As I mentioned earlier, Gandhi really did start something with his Salt March. Not only did he succeed, but his tactics also got so much attention that other resistance movements emulated and adapted them. We witnessed the same thing with Otpor's tactics, too. Activists in Georgia, Ukraine, Kyrgyzstan, Belarus, and Lebanon looked to us as models for their own resistance movements—and this process is ongoing. Imitation really is the sincerest form of flattery.

So how have things changed since Gandhi? One clear shift is in how movements communicate their message to the public. Technology, especially social media, has changed the landscape of the world's activism. How dilemma actions look—and what results they get—in the digital era is an important question with unexpectedly inspiring answers.

A hallmark of all activist creativity is that the action has unexpected or surprising developments. Today, results can be astonishing because an action might go viral. Very often what seems to be a lonely protest by a creative individual or small group can spark mass mobilization beyond expectations. Sometimes all it takes for successful mobilization is personal courage, powerful storytelling, and access to a social media account.

Let me give you an example that will surprise you.

One of the best examples of how technology can spark effective resistance comes to us from Zimbabwe. At the time of this action, Zimbabwe was a low-tech country ruled by a despot, Robert Mugabe, and its people faced historic levels of oppression, apathy, and fear. On April 20, 2016, Pastor Evan Mawarire made a Facebook post. In a four-minute inspirational video entitled "This Flag," Mawarire built on the poetics of anticolonial resistance and nationalization to create a rallying cry. In the video, Mawarire wears his country's flag while lamenting "the country's moribund economy, corruption, and human rights abuses."[13]

The video led to a hashtag #ThisFlag, which created a powerful bridge between social media and grassroots resistance. As the hashtag circulated, it helped draw attention to the repressive nature of the Mugabe regime and the urgent desire of those in Zimbabwe to break free of it. Even more important, a video posted on social media mobilized a recognizable local (and later international) protest movement against then-president Mugabe. In protests that were unprecedented in size and frequency, activists across Zimbabwe and internationally began using the Zimbabwean flag as a symbol for the resistance's "brand image." Sparked by a viral Facebook video, thousands of protesters took to the streets of Harare in the following months, demanding the departure of Robert Mugabe as president and accusing him of political misrule and economic mismanagement. The high visibility of the protests sparked international outrage when Zimbabwe's government arrested Mawarire and tried to press terrorism charges. But even though the government tried to repress Mawarire, it was too late to repress the uprising he sparked.

Facebook, Twitter, WhatsApp, and others may be useful tools, but these technologies still require a skilled strategic mind to guide their use. One excellent example of a deliberate dilemma action that creatively used technology took place recently in Spain. On April 10, 2015, No Somos Delito (We Are Not a Crime), a coalition of Spanish activist groups in Madrid, created a symbolic protest to raise awareness and to defend the obstruction of Spaniards' basic rights. Their democratic rights to freedom of expression, assembly, protest, and information were being limited by the Gag Law, also known as "La ley de seguridad ciudadana" (Citizen Safety Law). Under the Gag Law, protesting at certain locations would be considered a criminal act subject to a €30,000 fine. Because Spain was on the brink of a bitter and competitive election, the government really wanted to avoid news dominated by images of large crowds of protesters in front of the parliament building. Hence the Gag Law, which restricted public protest.

Undaunted, activists decided to create an alternative way to protest that allowed them to avoid being physically present in public places. Instead of going to a protest site, they created a hologram. Holograms for Freedom was a website for people around the globe, a portal for those who could not be physically present, to digitally protest in front of the Spanish Parliament. It allowed visitors to write or record their message on the website, which would then be projected in public.[14] The website attracted 800,000 people globally with 300,000 signing an online petition to abolish the law. The recordings were then projected, "the first hologram protest in history." Although this was a one-off digital protest, this dilemma action opened creative avenues for defending people's fundamental human rights. While the effort did not lead to overturning the law, the resistance gained momentum and let Spanish voices be heard by news media around the globe.

This range of examples offers a glimpse of the complex ways that dilemma actions can bring about political transformation. "Dimes for Change" was successful because no one got hurt, the authorities looked foolish, lots of regular people participated (perhaps for the first time), and the media

covered it widely. The TV-walking protest was pretty successful too, because it engaged a lot of people. Even though the
earlier curfew was a form of backlash, it only served to reduce
public support for the regime. #ThisFlag was extraordinarily
successful in drawing media coverage and using technology
to unite online efforts with grassroots, in-person organizing, though Mawarire went to jail. Perhaps more important,
all these regimes eventually fell, and these dilemma actions
played a critical role in advancing those changes. On the other
hand, the Holograms for Freedom did not change the law, but
it was a media triumph that engaged almost a billion people around the world. In other words, "success" is measured
variously, an inevitable phenomenon in complex movements
that are capable of eventually bringing about change.

The purpose of these all these actions—in different parts
of the world and for different kinds of struggles—is to create a
dilemma for the opponent whenever its policies conflict with
people's democratic rights, will, and common sense: such as
the beliefs that people should be able to make salt from the
ocean without paying the colonial government for it, or be
able to wear a hat, or sit at lunch counters, or express any of
these opinions in public. Through a long history of brilliant
and entertaining dilemma actions, strategists have forced
authoritarians to risk losing support no matter whether they
grant or deny the demands of nonviolent opposition.

Core Components of Dilemma Actions

So, the million-dollar questions are these: When are dilemma actions effective? Why? And what is the process behind designing a successful one? How do we measure efficacy? Is success only measured by the fall of a dictator? Or are there other ways to gauge success?

A core component of the tactics of dilemma actions is that they teach activists engaged in nonviolent struggles for democracy to think in ways that will allow them to succeed. Repressive regimes are successful, in large part, because they convince the population that they don't have alternatives and they don't have enough power to effect change. But our research on dilemma actions—and my personal history of training hundreds of activists worldwide in how to design them—proves that they *do* offer a path to systemic change. Planning dilemma actions shows activists how to use the hypocrisy, abuses of power, and intolerance of repressive leaders against them. Dilemma actions destabilize repression not just by revealing injustice and excess, but also by mocking the oppressor and showing its weaknesses—and ultimately undermining its authority. In other words, it's not only about inspiration and creativity, but about a *process*.

It is already clear that dilemma actions place an opponent in a situation where any response results in a humiliating outcome. In the designing process, nonviolent strategists clearly attempt to create a lose-lose framework for their opponent.

According to the CANVAS Core Curriculum and other literature, there are three core components of a good dilemma action.

1. Create or Identify a Rallying Issue Meaningful to the Public

Activists who have written about dilemma actions know that success in any of their manifestations requires paying attention to several critical elements. You have to know how the repressive power works, and you have to be savvy about winning hearts and minds.

You need to wisely choose the target of the dilemma action—that is, the beliefs and policies that the action will address. Both anecdotal evidence and research show that the most effective issues are usually related to government prohibitions or policies that intrude into people's personal lives, like the fact that citizens need salt and they don't want their government to regulate it. So, the first step in designing a dilemma action is to review the opponent's policies for burdensome restrictions on people's day-to-day activities. The more personal and intrusive those restrictions are, the bigger the dilemma will be for the opponent. This "review" doesn't mean spending hours in the library's basement archives or performing deep investigative journalism. Shadowy revelations are not the sort of policy we're looking for here. We mean the big, obvious, slap-in-the-face affronts, the ones that are already under everyone's noses. Create a shortlist of those.

Then, sort through them for the policies that run counter to widely held beliefs, even among the opponent's supporters. Think, for example, of the simplicity of refusing to give up your seat on a bus. When Rosa Parks chose to do that, she easily called attention to the outrage of segregationist policy.

2. Design the Action

I dentify an action that will put the opponent in a position of either granting the nonviolent movement an exemption to the restrictions or engaging in unpopular sanctions. As with any successful nonviolent tactic, your dilemma action plan should minimize risks and boost possible benefits within your specific social, cultural, religious, and media environment. In one of the most comprehensive academic analyses to date, "The Dilemma Action: Analysis of an Activist Technique," Majken Jul Sørensen and Brian Martin identify five factors common to dilemma actions that have forced opponents into a tough spot, thus representing a "to-do list" for designing dilemma actions[15]:

1. *The action needs a constructive, positive element*, such as delivering humanitarian aid.
2. *Activists should use surprise or unpredictability*, such as staging a protest with holograms instead of live people.
3. *Opponents' prime choices should be in different domains* (political, social, personal), *which means that the choices are difficult to compare.* When a police officer has to choose whether or not to arrest a nonviolent protester at a demonstration doing something funny and popular, for example, there is a conflict between the economic (keep the job) and the social (agree with the protester) domains.
4. *Dilemma actions should seek a timing that appeals to mass media coverage, making it difficult for authorities to ignore*, such as including an element of humor or a prank the way that the Yes Men did when they impersonated Dow Chemical, which makes it fun for media to cover.
5. *Appealing to widely held beliefs increases pressure*, such as appealing to society's basic idea that governments shouldn't tell you that you can't wear a particular type of hat.

Additionally, there are dilemma actions that backfire, and understanding what makes them backfire is essential. Our research shows that some dilemma actions can also divide audiences and cause backlash for the group by alienating potential supporters. Think of the well-known "Punk Prayer" performed by Russian dissident band Pussy Riot on February 12, 2012, in Moscow's Church of Christ the Savior. On one hand, it resulted in a lot of visibility and a sought-after, outsized response from the opponent; it also leveraged the widely held belief (even in very conservative societies) that religious institutions should function apart from the state and its party politics. Yet on the other hand, because Pussy Riot decided to perform their political action inside an actual church building, it was easy for their opponent to label their provocation as "anti-religious" and "insulting to those who believe." This made it easy for the target of Pussy Riot's actions to stoke nationwide outrage against the punk band. So as in the example of how the national anthem kneeling protests of NFL players led to debates about signaling patriotism rather than police brutality, the Pussy Riot protest similarly led to an uproar over their disrespect for religion rather than a desired debate on the role of religious institutions in politics and society. This blowback underscores why it is essential to carefully plan and design each aspect of the dilemma action in order to measure its potential impact and possible interpretations.

The best way to avoid blowback is to have a strong sense of the various examples of dilemma actions and their outcomes. While we share a selection of dilemma actions throughout this essay, there are many more examples to draw from. The best way to ensure that your dilemma action will be successful is to study similar examples so you can compare them to your specific context and gauge the fit. For a good resource on dilemma actions, we recommend *Beautiful Trouble: A Toolbox for Revolution,* a collaborative effort edited by Andrew Boyd and Dave Oswald Mitchell that brings together dozens of seasoned artists and activists from around the world to distill their best practices of "decision dilemmas" into a toolbox for creative action. Published first in 2016, it is also a website that is constantly updated with new examples of case studies, principles, tactics, practitioners, and theory.[16]

If you want even more ideas, you can also look at the "Global Nonviolent Action Database," which offers free access to hundreds of completed examples of nonviolent action.[17] All of this work by activists offers inspiration as you think about how best to devise a struggle for democracy. We may have slightly different tactics we emphasize, but all theories of dilemma actions have a common thread: force the government to be stuck in a dilemma where if they do nothing to stop the protesters, they look bad, and if they do something to stop them, they look even worse.

3. Perform the Action and Benefit from Its Outcome

If you've been savvy about Steps 1 and 2, you will probably have selected some very unpopular individuals—stakeholders and "public faces" of unpopular restrictions, policies, or practices within the oppressive system—who personalize the dilemma action. That means the opponent is likely to react, and if that reaction is strong enough, it will undermine your opponent's legitimacy.

While it is best to identify a public figure who embodies what you are resisting, it is also wise to add celebrities to your ranks if you can. When actors, sports personalities, thought leaders, or local community leaders participate in the action, they raise its profile and thus directly influence its outcome. People identify with role models, and if these personalities show up, many more people will usually follow.

We tried it ourselves in Serbia. A famous Serbian actor, Voja Brajović, finished a very popular performance in the Serbian National Theatre in late 1999. For this performance, he replaced his usual shirt with a T-shirt with the fist symbol of the Otpor movement, handed to him earlier by Otpor activists. Wearing this symbol in public was strictly prohibited, and average activists—even including high school kids—were regularly detained for wearing it. But when a public figure like Brajović wore the symbol, the police were too confused to interrupt the show, and arresting one of the most prominent actors in Serbia on the stage would have been too costly even for Milošević's regime. Days later, actors and musicians repeated this action all over Serbia, setting brave personal examples for average citizens who were—until then—regularly arrested for wearing this symbol in public and therefore afraid to take risks. Creative and well-planned action increases the costs of intervention for your opponent and reduces the risks and costs of disobedience for ordinary people.

Once a dilemma action is performed, many of the groups in our study added another step. This follow-up step, which we commonly described in my Otpor days as "post-production of the tactic," aims not only to build on the immediate outcome, but also to exploit the opponent's response to the action by gaining as many press mentions, views, and new supporters as possible. There is a range of ways to draw attention to a successful action and use it to build your ranks, but the most important one is to make sure that the media's coverage of your story continues. For instance, have your own Twitter army keep using a hashtag or form connections with recognized journalists. Activating this step means having a follow-up media plan *before* you begin your action.

The goal is always to encourage more people to support the nonviolent movement. Bigger numbers help you. As you draw attention to your action—showing the public how you put your opponent in a dilemma in a peaceful and socially supportive way—you help show that your vision is not a radical threat to society, but, rather, that your target is the real threat. More people will join your struggle. And, of course, as the next section explains, one excellent way to win people's hearts and minds is to add the component of humor to your dilemma action, because the media can't resist covering stories where those in power are made to look silly or stupid.

Laughtivism: The Secret Ingredient

Dilemma actions can also be humorous. But are they even more successful? Let's face it—for the most part, resistance to repression is serious business. But as we learned in Serbia, you can really advance your serious cause if you add some humor.

If it goes against common assumptions that nonviolence is more effective than violent protests, try making the argument that using humor is more effective in a political struggle than being angry. The idea of using humor to advance a cause often seems to contradict assumptions about the role of comedy in politics. The common assumption is that, if you are laughing, you might be venting frustration or mocking an abusive power, but you can't possibly be making a difference. At least that was the idea. But there is now proof that laughtivism is actually a positive component of successful nonviolent activism. When you insert an element of play, you melt fear and you unmask authority's weaknesses.

But don't take our word for it. We have growing evidence of why laughtivism is so successful.[18] Majken Jul Sørensen studied it, and in *Humour in Political Activism: Creative Nonviolent Resistance*, she describes five different types of humorous political stunts.[19] What they all have in common is that they help the public laugh at abusive authority. Laughing inverts a power dynamic and reduces fear. Suddenly it is the ones laughing who have the power because they can see the flaws in the system. Once that happens, the movement will gain steam.

Sarah Freeman-Woolpert, a former CANVAS intern and student of mine from Harvard, explains this idea in detail in her article in "Waging Nonviolence." She writes, "Using humor and irony to undermine white supremacy dates back to the days of the Third Reich, from jokes and cartoons employed by Norwegians against the Nazi occupation to 'The Great Dictator' speech by Charlie Chaplin."[20] In recent years, we have seen a resurgence in Nazis—and likewise of laughtivism to counter them. Today, the resistance takes the unlikely form of clowns—troupes of brightly dressed activists who show up to neo-Nazi gatherings and make a public mockery of their hateful messages. This puts white supremacists in a dilemma: their own use of violence will seem unwarranted, yet their machismo image is tainted by the comedic performance.

Humor deescalates their rallies, turning what could become a violent confrontation into a big joke. Cases show that anti-Nazi clowning can also turn into a wider community event, bringing local people together in solidarity and fun.

For instance, take the recent, mocking response to far-right demonstrators in the German town of Wunsiedel. One of the cases we studied highlights an "involuntary walk-a-thon" organized in response to an annual neo-Nazi march. The organizers drew chalk markers on the pavement marking the starting point, halfway point, and finish line. Residents and local businesses pledged to donate ten euros for every meter the white supremacists marched to a group called EXIT Deutschland, which is dedicated to helping people leave right-wing extremist groups. People came out to cheer the marchers the day of the event, flanking the route with signs that read, "If only the Fuhrer knew!" and "Mein Mamph!" (or "My Munch") by a table of bananas offered to the walkers. This turned the marchers into involuntary resistors of their own cause and brought the community together in unity to counter the messages of white supremacy.

Other European cities have employed clowns to counter the anti-immigrant groups that seem to be ballooning under the recent wave of populist politics. For example, the "Loldiers of Odin" formed in Finland to counter a citizen patrol called Soldiers of Odin.[21] The clowns danced around the streets the same nights that the patrols went out in the community, bringing acrobat hoops and a hobby horse. They also danced around the "soldiers" while playing in the snow. Their actions countered right-wing propaganda of making the streets "safer" from immigrants by bringing humor and silliness to their actions.

These cases show in astonishing ways how dilemma actions and laughtivism are equally effective against hate-mongers, racists, and xenophobic extremists as they are against authoritarians.

How Humor Works

The best acts of laughtivism confront their opponent with a dilemma. The government can *react* to those who ridicule it—detaining people, confiscating objects that were part of the action, or even processing and sentencing practitioners—thereby making themselves look even more ridiculous in the process. Or it can *ignore the acts* of laughtivism aimed against them, thereby opening the floodgates of dissent and enabling numerous replicas of the original action.

Indeed, when faced with an act of brazen mockery, oppressive regimes and strongmen have no good choices. Whatever they do, they will likely be perceived as losers. And that is because authoritarian power has no sense of humor. In the United States, you might make fun of the president, like for example when Chevy Chase impersonated Gerald Ford

on Saturday Night Live (SNL) or Jordan Peele impersonated Barack Obama. In those cases, if the president doesn't
react strongly and even jokes about the impersonation, then
it doesn't have a major negative effect on public perceptions
of the person mocked. But, in contrast, if you have a strong,
negative reaction, as Donald Trump did when Alec Baldwin
impersonated him for SNL or in reaction to Sarah Cooper's
TikTok impersonations, you open yourself up to even more
mockery. As a result, whenever Trump tweets his displeasure
at comedians, other high-profile comedians along with the
general public respond by making fun of him.

But that's just an example from a Western democracy. It
works elsewhere, too. Take as another example Putin's Russia,
where instead of ignoring the prank—and being perceived
as weak—the regime was forced to act and ended up looking bizarre and stupid. In early 2012—after local authorities
barred public demonstrations that brought thousands in the
streets in the aftermath of an election scandal—activists from
the Siberian city of Barnaul staged a "toy protest."[22] Instead of
carrying anti-Putin placards themselves, which would most
probably get them immediately detained, Russian laughtivists propped up teddy bears, Lego characters, and South Park
figurines to carry their messages for them. The toy protest
backed Kremlin authorities into an awkward rationalization
for banning something as seemingly inconsequential as a
Lego toy holding a sign? After confiscating the unsanctioned
toy "protesters," Siberian authorities placed an official ban on

all future toy protests because the toys were not Russian citizens, but were, in fact, made in China. Thanks to the government's clumsy reaction, videos, images, and stories of their decision made national and international headlines.

Laughtivism even works against an oppressive military junta. The Burmese military faced hundreds of thousands of demonstrators with live rounds and tanks and did not hesitate to slaughter hundreds of them in cold blood during the Saffron Revolution in 2007. But just a year later, the regime was caught off guard and internationally humiliated by ladies' undergarments. The "Panties for Peace" campaign "played on the weaknesses of their opponents by exploiting the belief held by many in the military junta that female undergarments would drain power from the military regime by cursing their soldiers."[23] While the idea that they would be scared of panties may seem silly, to them it was a legitimate fear. So activists decided to play on this weakness and for more than ten months, women in Burma and from around the world mailed their panties to local Burmese embassies and to members of the military in a bid to strip the regime of its power and bring an end to its gross violations of human rights, especially those committed against Burma's women. With no clear answer to the creative provocation of these "laughtivists," the Burmese ruling generals *just abstained from reacting.* Normally wary Burmese women grew more confident, and other human rights groups gained motivation to escalate their campaign and replicate it both domestically and internationally.

You may doubt that the laughtivist approach leads to sustained political change. After all, if they are to succeed, activists must convey meanings and deliver messages, not just pull off a pratfall or a sight gag. But there is a reason humor is such a popular tool in the modern activist's arsenal: it works. For one thing, it breaks fear and builds confidence. For another, it also adds the necessary "cool factor," which helps movements attract new members. Additionally, much laughtivism can be done electronically using the tools available via digital media to call attention to abuses of power. Memes, for example, are easy to create and even easier to circulate, allowing users and sharers the relative safety of anonymity. Finally, humor does an excellent job of posing a dilemma for your opponent that tends to lead to clumsy reactions. The best acts of laughtivism clearly force autocrats and their security pillars into lose-lose scenarios, undermining the credibility of their regimes or institutions no matter how they manage to respond.

There may be another, more psychological reason why laughtivism works, especially against the mighty and powerful. Politicians, whether democratically elected or having seized power through other means, usually share an inflated sense of self-importance. After too long in power, and after seeing their own photoshopped face too many times in newspapers and on the covers of magazines, they inevitably start living in a kind of unreality. It's as if they start believing their own propaganda, and as a result, they start *taking themselves too seriously.* This is why they very often react viscerally and in a self-defeating way when challenged with laughtivism.

And, as we have argued, one of the critical reasons why laughtivism is so effective is that it helps point out the situational irony of abusive power.[24] When a dictator claims that he is operating in the public's interest by repressing them, that situation is ironic, even if it isn't funny. The situation is ironic because it holds deep structural contradictions. It claims to be good for the public when in essence it is bad. It is like the shiny, happy photos of dictators that tend to line highways or show up in political advertisements. Their smiles make you cringe. Laughtivists are in a unique position to use critical irony to expose these flaws, unmask the farce, and show that the emperor, in fact, has no clothes. Once a resistance movement learns how to analyze the ironic contradictions of a repressive system, they can then find creative and entertaining ways to expose it.[25]

For example, if a government is using excessive force but telling the public that force is needed to "keep the peace," then all protesters need to do is emphasize their peacefulness in order to show that the force is unnecessarily repressive. If, for example, the protesters hold out a flower like a gun in the face of police in riot gear, the flower will immediately allow the public to see the painful irony of their government's guns. And if the protesters hold flowers while dressed as clowns, it will show the public that the government has manufactured the threat that they supposedly need to repress. Suddenly the laughtivists have shown that the real threat is a violent government and the protesters are not dangerous at all—and even better, such an action shows that they are so confident in their views that they can make jokes about those in power. That sort of attitude helps attract support for the cause and turn the tide.

Of course, just because laughter in nonviolent struggles has recently become so common, it is not easy or "spontaneous." On the contrary, research shows laughtivism, as a special form of dilemma action, requires a similar set of strategic components to prepare, design, and perpetuate a constant stream of creativity to stay in the news, headlines, and tweets, as well as to maintain a movement's momentum. As explained above, a key element of a successful dilemma action is a communications strategy. This is true for laughtivism, too. You can make power look like a joke, but you can't assume that the media will cover the story without your calling attention to it. Once the media is aware, though, the chances are even higher that they will help draw even more attention.

The challenges to successful laughtivism are worth the gain. Humorous political stunts, like the ones in Sørensen's study and in ours, attract new members, get media attention, and facilitate dialogue. Of course, there are risks to adding humor to resistance movements—especially the risk of not being taken seriously by the public or further dividing society. The risk of violent reprisals is real too. Even though nonviolent actions tend to protect those who wage them, it is important to note that when laughtivism incites a violent response, this response may be even more aggressive than in actions that do not include laughtivism. This is so because when a figure and its allies feel mocked and dehumanized the results can be highly toxic. This was the case, for example, in the attacks on the French satirical magazine *Charlie Hebdo*.[26] Taking those risks into consideration, however, there are still many good reasons for activists to use laughtivism.

By and large, we find that when humor is a component of dilemma actions, it is an especially valuable weapon against repression. If you thought it was hard to arrest protesters being peaceful, it is way harder to arrest them when they are dressed as clowns or they are making out in a subway.

A Proven Tactic

Dilemma actions can also be referred to as dilemma decisions or dilemma demonstrations, depending on the specific action the group chooses. Regardless of which version you employ, the common denominator is the goal of putting your opponent between a rock and a hard place. I know from experience that dilemma actions, if tailored correctly to the context and conducted well, succeed. I've done it. I've seen it. I've taught others how to do it.

And I'm not alone.

Other activists have written accounts of these types of actions, including George Lakey, whose *Powerful Peacemaking: A Strategy for a Living Revolution* offered an early account of "dilemma demonstrations" back in 1973.[27] Philippe Duhamel, a Canadian activist, explains that he devised what he calls a dilemma demonstration after reading Lackey's work. Duhamel's *The Dilemma Demonstration: Using*

Nonviolent Civil Disobedience to Put the Government between a Rock and a Hard Place presents a series of effective components to a dilemma demonstration.[28] Yet while the practice of dilemma actions may have a storied history, we haven't tried *learning* from them for very long. If we are going to promote dilemma actions as an effective and productive tactic for advancing democracy, we should know what we are doing, right?

Scholars have begun to assess the strengths, risks, core components, and success rates of dilemma actions. We are currently engaged in a major quantitative study of the effects of dilemma actions, and we offer some primary results here.

Our Research Results

The forty-four cases our team researched come from five continents and encompass the years 1930–2019. Almost half of our selected cases include elements of humor (laughtivism) as a key part of their dilemma action's strategic framework. Because we wanted to explore dilemma actions in different contexts and environments, we chose cases that covered a wide array of issues, ranging from basic human rights (e.g., freedom of speech and assembly), prodemocracy struggles, and activism for gender and social equality, as well as struggles against corruption and for self-determination. We also wanted to look at diverse political and democratic contexts for dilemma action tactics. So, in addition to many brilliant examples of dilemma activism that operated in hostile environments and challenged well-known autocrats, we also examined several recent cases where dilemma actions tackled issues of racial disparity, economic equality, and immigrant rights in the countries largely considered to be democracies, such as the United States and Europe.

In the appendix, you will find the full list of cases we used for this preliminary study organized by date. We used a binary metric to measure the categories for each case. We applied a set of nine questions for each case to determine the success of each question, allowing us to categorize the outcome as, "Yes, it did succeed," "No, it did not succeed," or, "N/A, to indicate unknown." The questions applied for this preliminary study are the following:

- Did it attract media attention?[29]
- Did it reduce fear and apathy among activists?
- Did it attract more supporters?
- Did it reduce risk of severe punishment to activists, or in cases of an oppressive response by authority, make the punishment backfire?[30]
- Did it allow activists to reframe the opponent's narrative, changing their image from "powerful or scary" to "laughable or vincible?"
- Was the action later replicated and spread across constituencies or geography?

- Was there an international reaction?
- Were there resignations or public excuses from target officials or institutions?
- Did it involve elements of "laughtivism?"

Overall, we found a remarkable degree of success, as shown in table 1.

Table 1: Preliminary assessment of the effects of dilemma actions

Question	All cases	Laughtivism only
Did the dilemma action attract media attention?	98%	100%
Did it reduce fear and apathy among activists?	80%	80%
Did it reduce risk of severe punishment to activists, and in case of oppressive answer, make it backfire?	60%	60%
Did it attract more supporters?	81%	67%
Did it allow activists to reframe the narrative of the opponent—from "powerful" or "scary" to "laughable or vincible?"	58%	81%
Was it later replicated and spread across constituencies or geography?	74%	75%
Was there an international reaction?	49%	38%
Was there resignation or public excuses from target officials or institutions?	45%	43%
Did it involve elements of "laughtivism"?	48%	100%

It's important to say, the numbers above are early research—but they are promising. They begin to tell us some things we want to know and also raise some good questions for activists who are considering their next move. For instance, why would laughtivism be *less* likely to attract new supporters, if it results in *more* media attention? We'll get to that in a minute. Suffice to say here, though, that these early results must be qualified by our relatively small sample size. Also, our media coverage numbers (98 percent of all cases we looked at!) probably suffer from a sampling bias: that is, we know about the action because it was reported. There are many other less-well-covered actions we are excited to study, and we will do so in future research.

Now, on to the results. One important finding is that the study corroborates the kinds of success that you have heard about or experienced yourself when using these tactics. We find alignment between subjective and object realities, and that's good.

Among the forty-four dilemma actions we studied, 80 percent resulted in a reduction of fear and apathy among activists, 60 percent reduced the risk of severe punishment, and 98 percent attracted substantial media attention. Around 81 percent of the cases attracted more members; 58 percent of them effectively reframed the narrative; and 74 percent were successively replicated. On those metrics that seemed to indicate less favorability for dilemma actions, such as the fact that 49 percent provoked an international reaction and

43 percent resulted in concessions by target officials, those numbers still represent significant success. In fact, they demonstrate a success rate that outpaces violent resistance success rates (which are 23 percent) by a ratio of almost two to one.[31]

Now, what about laughtivism? On many measures, laughtivism and dilemma actions overall have similar results, and laughtivism was highly successful in general. All twenty-one laughtivism cases drew substantial media attention. Eighty percent of them reduced fear among activists, and 60 percent reduced the risk of punishment—numbers identical to dilemma actions overall. What we found most interesting were those metrics where laughtivism and nonhumorous dilemma actions diverge. What we found, and what conforms to anecdotal experience, is that laughtivism is extremely successful at reframing the narrative (81 percent success versus 58 percent for all cases), even if it might be a little less successful at attracting new members (67 percent versus 81 percent for all cases).

This makes sense. Spectators to laughtivism might participate in a public prank but not feel that they can easily join the movement. Maybe they are more introverted or don't think they have a good sense of humor, or they perceive the activist group to be closed. (Or they fear that the target authority might lash out because it's being mocked.) But because laughtivism uses critical irony to reveal the situational irony of repression, it is extremely good at changing how the public thinks.

For example, when the Indivisible campaign, a response to the election of Donald Trump, decided to highlight the lack of congressional accountability to constituents, they devised a brilliant plan to hold town meetings where missing representatives were depicted by empty suits, cardboard cutouts, and in one case, a chicken. This tactic made it incredibly clear to the public that their political representatives were out of touch. It used the irony of representing politicians as missing to underscore the irony that their elected officials were too "busy" or "scared" to talk to voters. This is also a good example of a tactic that did draw more members—possibly because the tactics felt easy for anyone to employ. If activists were dressed as clowns, in other words, the more performative nature of the action might cause many would-be activists to shy away from the thought of putting on a crazy wig and red nose. (The clowns in other actions, however, were great at reframing the narrative and being replicated by other activists already in the cause.)

Finally, bear one more thing in mind. Dilemma actions are a piece of a bigger picture: a spark that takes a movement to another level, or else a single tactic used by an established group. Isolating these tactics, as we've done, does not account for times when international attention or concessions were granted to a movement at a later date or in response to the ways that the dilemma action helped a group increase its visibility and membership. It's hard to fully capture all the ways that the dilemma action might help a group increase its visibility and membership, and our research is just beginning.

Conclusion

By looking at forty-four dilemma actions under a microscope, we found that they are more likely to succeed if they create a public issue *either* out of the absence of a reaction by the opponent *or* because of a clumsy, possibly repressive reaction when a nonviolent group is breaking one of its laws. If it is possible, the skillful use of media (including social media platforms like Facebook, Twitter, and Instagram) is an effective amplifier, as happened in the examples of Indivisible or No Somos Delito (We Are Not a Crime).

What we have learned from the research and case studies is a need to carefully adapt the core elements of dilemma actions to a range of cultural contexts and in response to a range of repressive regimes. In the age of social media, successful tactics are often shared between activists coming from various struggles "horizontally" (with no mentoring, training, or education from a third party). Successful (and sometimes very creative) cases of dilemma actions often serve as role models or inspiration for movements operating in very different contexts and very distant parts of the globe. But we should be wary of just "copy-pasting" a tactic from one context to another. It is essential to make sure that in each case, the dilemma action has been carefully adapted to the specific situation. This is even more important when groups add an element of humor, mocking, or political satire to the design process. What might be funny and fun in one context could be offensive and disrespectful in another.

So how do we learn from successes and failures, and then apply what we learned?

As we've said, our goal was to move beyond experience and anecdote and theory into proof. The recent rise of right-wing politics, growing illiberalism, and xenophobia has demanded a growing struggle to hold these democracies accountable to their supposed ideals. We now have proof that dilemma actions work in this cause. As a subset of nonviolent resistance movements, they can significantly help a group advance its calls for democracy. We have also explained the specific elements of a successful dilemma action, offering a contribution to social movements across the globe.

Our research clearly shows the amazing potential of dilemma actions as a strategic tool to tackle human rights abuses, autocracy, injustice, and inequality. Not only are dilemma actions more likely to grant their organizers visibility and a possibility for mobilization, but they also often inspire other local and international actors to replicate those tactics.[32] In two-thirds of the cases we studied, other movements replicated the tactics. More often than not, the response from the opponent was self-compromising, giving organizers a window to follow the original action up with secondary tactics or protests. The creative and strategic processes behind organizing dilemma actions are vital, and we will continue to share our findings with the world.

Two things keep democracy and freedom alive: strong institutions and active citizens. It is a two-way street. Institutions must serve their citizens, and citizens must in turn defend democratic institutions from abuse. Plenty of movements and organizations across the globe are challenging their autocratic governments with courage and creativity. In this time of democratic backsliding, we see that Americans and Europeans may have taken democracy for granted for too long.[33] Those of us who have taken part in civil resistance movements in the past know all too well that authoritarians depend on apathy. Apathy, though, also plagues democracies. Our finding that over 60 percent of dilemma actions attracted new members suggests that these sorts of tactics can pull many citizens out of apathy and into engagement.

And that's where you come in. Remember that sharing your experiences helps inspire others and sharpen their strategies. The bottom line is that democracy is simply too serious a matter to be left to politicians or parties alone. And grassroots campaigning is more effective when it's fun. Oligarchs, just like autocrats, are weakened when they become objects of derision. Together, we have every reason to research, study, and practice dilemma actions and laughtivism in prodemocracy struggles. It may be the best direct remedy for challenging authoritarians and defending our democracies at home.

Appendix

Chronological List of Case Studies

	Year	Location	Title	Activist group	Target	Summary	Type of struggle
1	1930	India	Salt March	Mahatma Gandhi	British rulers	Gandhi and his followers walked for three weeks, producing salt from ocean water in opposition to the strict British taxes on it.	Prodemocracy
2	1938	Washington, DC	Cherry Tree Rebellion		Jefferson Memorial Relocation Project	Activists opposed the relocation of the Jefferson Memorial by padlocking themselves to the cherry trees, wresting shovels from the workers' hands, and throwing dirt back into the holes.	Environmental

3	1955–6	Montgomery, AL	Montgomery Bus Boycott	Rosa Parks	Segregation norms in the public transportation system	After an African American woman refused to give up her bus seat for a white person, thousands of black citizens of Montgomery refused to ride city buses until they were desegregated.	Racial equality
4	1960	Nashville, TN	Lunch counter sit-ins	Nashville Student Movement and the Nashville Christian Leadership Council	Jim Crow South	Black students took seats at all-white lunch counters, refusing to move until the segregation laws were changed.	Racial equality
5	1969; 1986–1991	Estonia	Singing Revolution		USSR Occupational Authorities	A choir sang patriotic songs previously banned by the Soviet authorities at the most popular music festival in the country. The audience joined in, and they could not be drowned out.	Prodemocracy

(continued)

Year	Location	Title	Activist group	Target	Summary	Type of struggle
6 1971	Chile	Cacerolazo		Salvador Allende and his government	Citizens protested widespread hunger by marching through the streets of Santiago banging empty pans, kettles, and stew pots with spoons to create noise and disturbance.	Accountability
7 1977	Argentina	Damas de la Plaza de Mayo Argentina	The Madres of Plaza de Mayo	Argentina's government	The mothers of the young people who were tortured and killed walked in a nonviolent demonstration in front of the Argentine government site.	Prodemocracy

8	1978	New Zealand	Tree sitting	Steven King and Shirley Guildford	Government logging policies	Activists protested logging activities by building platforms and tree houses on large trees and physically occupying the area, preventing them from being cut down.	Environmental
9	1980	Norway	Kampanjen Mot Verneplikt	Kampanjen Mot Verneplikt	Norwegian government	A network of antiwar objectors staged "jail-ins" where they would arrive at a prison and demand that other objectors be freed or they all be jailed.	Prodemocracy
10	1983	Chile	Anti-Pinochet slow-down	Coalition of labor unions	Mass disruption of traffic and transport	Citizens walked or drove very slowly on designated days, bringing many cities to literal halts in a way that the regime could not retaliate against.	Prodemocracy

(continued)

	Year	Location	Title	Activist group	Target	Summary	Type of struggle
11	1987	Poland	Orange Alternative	Orange Alternative, led by Waldemar Fydrych	The communist regime	Absurdist organized street happenings were used to ridicule the Communist regime, including distributing toilet paper, sanitary towels, and pretzels to passersby, singing Stalinist hymns while holding hands around the orangutan cage at the Warsaw Zoo, and leading a march of 10,000 people in orange dwarf hats.	Prodemocracy

					Accountability
12	1998	United States	Whose Tea Party?	United for a Fair Economy	Republican Party	Two protesters paddled in a small boat, with a sign "Working Family Life Raft," in the harbor next to where the Republican Party was announcing new tax initiatives that would hurt working families.
13	1999	Belgrade, Serbia	Arresting an oil barrel	Otpor!	Slobodan Milošević	Passersby were encouraged to hit an oil barrel with the unpopular prime minister's face on it before it was taken away by police.	Prodemocracy

(continued)

	Year	Location	Title	Activist group	Target	Summary	Type of struggle
14	2001	Canada	Operation SalAMI		Canadian government	After the government refused to hand over drafts of a trade agreement, activists barricaded the office, performing what they called a "search and seizure" until they agreed to release the document.	Accountability
15	2002	online	The Yes Men (WTO)	The Yes Men	World Trade Organization (WTO)	A fake website is created where activists pose as the World Trade Organization, only to be invited to large conferences where they pull satirical stunts.	Accountability

	Year	Place	Campaign	Organization	Target	Description	Theme
16	2004	Online	The Yes Men (Fake Press)	The Yes Men	Dow Chemical	The Yes Men pretended to be a Dow Chemical representative and went on BBC and accepted full responsibility for the 1984 Bhopal tragedy.	Accountability
17	2005	Ukraine	Remember About the Gas		Russian Federation	Ukraine activists promoted a boycott of Russian goods amid the 2005 gas conflict by passing out leaflets with the phrase "Remember about the Gas—do not buy Russian goods!"	Accountability
18	2007	Myanmar	Panties for Peace	Lanna Action for Burma Party	Leading generals of the ruling military junta	Women from around the world sent their underwear in the mail to local Burmese embassies in a bid to strip the regime of its power.	Human rights

(continued)

	Year	Location	Title	Activist group	Target	Summary	Type of struggle
19	2007	United States	Clowns vs. Nazis #1	Coup Cluts Clowns	KKK members and other neofascists	A group calling themselves the "Coup Cluts Clowns" put themselves in opposition to a KKK rally by dressing up in clownish outfits and satirizing the neo-Nazis.	Racial equality
20	2007	Maldives	Rice Pudding for Democracy		Maldivian Democratic Party (MDP)	Activists hosted "rice pudding parties" where people could eat their national dish while openly talking politics with present opposition activists.	Prodemocracy

21	2009	Iran	Chanting from the rooftops		Ayatollah Khamenei and his regime	Iranians would go on their rooftops at night and chant "Allahu akbar" (God is great) as a symbolic expression to show their opposition to the regime.	Prodemocracy
22	2010	Gaza	Freedom Flotilla	Free Gaza Movement	Israeli and Egyptian governments	A convoy filled with well-known activists, journalists, and humanitarian aid challenged the blockade of the Gaza Strip, but were fatally raided, drawing backlash.	Accountability
23	2011	Belarus	Silent protests		Alexander Lukashenko (Belarussian president)	Knowing that chanting slogans would land them in jail, people dissatisfied with Belarus's government would instead clap to show opposition.	Prodemocracy

(*continued*)

	Year	Location	Title	Activist group	Target	Summary	Type of struggle
24	2011	Egypt	Protest at Tahrir Square		Hosni Mubarak and his government	Thousands of Egyptian citizens gathered in a symbolic public space, demanding Mubarak's resignation. They sang songs of freedom and spoke in favor of a political change for the country, saying they would not leave until he resigned.	Prodemocracy
25	2011	Uganda	Walk-to-work protests	Activists for Change	Yoweri Museveni's government	Opposition politicians and their supporters took a stand against spiraling food and fuel prices by walking to work.	Accountability

26	2012	Barnaul, Russia	Toy protest	Golos	Vladimir Putin and the Russian government	Unable to obtain their own permits, activists lined up toys holding their antigovernment signs.	Prodemocracy
27	2012	Russia	Pussy Riot	Pussy Riot	Russian Orthodox Church; Putin as a secondary target	Feminist punk band Pussy Riot staged a concert inside a Moscow cathedral. They were arrested and jailed for two years, drawing a huge international reaction.	Prodemocracy
28	2012	Russia	Pothole Politicians	Make Officials Work	Local officials	To get their potholes fixed, activists painted mocking caricatures of local officials around the holes, transforming them into comically grotesque mouths.	Accountability

(continued)

	Year	Location	Title	Activist group	Target	Summary	Type of struggle
29	2012	Ukraine	FEMEN	FEMEN	Church in general; Russian oppressive government	In solidarity with Pussy Riot, activists cut down a cross in central Kyiv in opposition to the government and its connection with the church	Prodemocracy
30	2012	Montenegro	Underwear protest	Network for Affirmation of the Nongovernmental Sector (MANS)	Prime Minister Igor Lukšić	MANS strung up underwear in front of the government building in Podgorica with the names of government officials pinned to them.	Accountability
31	2013	Ankara, Turkey	Kisses in the subway		Turkish government	After one couple was chastised for kissing in public, hundreds of couples flooded Turkey's subways to do the same thing.	Accountability

32	2013	Turkey	The Standing Man	Erdem Gündüz	Turkish government	Erdem Gündüz stood in silence in Taksim Square, staring at a statue of the founder of modern Turkey. He was eventually joined by a large crowd and the idea of "the standing man" spread around the globe.	Prodemocracy
33	2014	Thailand	Sandwiches for Democracy	Thai Student Centre for Democracy	Military junta	Student activists handed out "sandwiches for democracy," in the time when gatherings of five or more people were banned.	Prodemocracy
34	2014	Germany	Clowns vs. Nazis #2		Neofascist pilgrims	A town popular with Nazi sympathizers turned a planned rally into a mock sporting event, raising money for every meter walked by the neo-Nazis.	Racial equality

(continued)

	Year	Location	Title	Activist group	Target	Summary	Type of struggle
35	2014	Cuba	Painted Pigs	Danilo Maldonado "El Sexto"	Castro brothers	A popular graffiti artist hatched the perfect scheme: he would release two pigs in a public space, one painted with "Fidel" and the other "Raul." However, he was arrested and detained before he could carry it out.	Prodemocracy
36	2014	Taiwan	Sunflower Student Movement		China and Legislative and Executive Yuan of Taiwan	A group of students and civic groups occupied the Chinese legislature in Taiwan, opposing a trade bill between China and Taiwan.	Prodemocracy

37	2015	Spain	Holograms for Freedom	No Somos Delito	Spanish government	Recorded messages of people from around the world expressing their grievances with the Spanish government were projected in front of the Spanish Parliament.	Prodemocracy
38	2016	Zimbabwe	#ThisFlag	Pastor Ewan Mawarire	Autocratic and corrupt government	Zimbabwe citizens used the hashtag #ThisFlag on social media to post messages to the leading party, racking up countless hits.	Accountability
39	2016	Finland 2016	Clowns vs. Nazis #3	Loldiers of Odin	Soldiers of Odin	An activist group dressed as clowns, dancing and singing to oppose a popular anti-immigration group's silent protest.	Racial equality

(continued)

	Year	Location	Title	Activist group	Target	Summary	Type of struggle
40	2016–18	Iran	Women attend football		Conservative government; Ministry of Sport	Iran women got around being banned from attending football matches by dressing up as men and sharing it on social media.	Gender equality
41	2017	United States	Indivisible	Indivisible	Tea Party politics and the Trump administration	The Indivisible Activist group created a step-by-step guide to bring down the Trump platform using tactics from the Tea Party.	Prodemocracy
42	2018	Harare, Zimbabwe	Potholes to Garden Beds	Vision Africa and Better Bulawayo Initiative	Pothole issues	Activists filled potholes with trees to force the local government to take action and fix them.	Accountability

| 43 | 2019 | Kazakhstan | Empty Signs and Full Prosecution | Aslan Sagutdinox | Aslan Sagutdinox | A man held up a blank sign in a public square to criticize a lack of free speech. The video of him being arrested went viral. | Prodemocracy |
| 44 | 2019 | New York City | #NoKidsInCages | The Refugee and Immigrant Center for Education and Legal Services | Trump administration | Employing a guerilla marketing strategy, activists set up artistic replicas of children in cages on the sidewalks of New York City. | Human rights |

Notes

1 Founded in 2003 and headquartered in Belgrade, the Centre for Applied Nonviolent Action and Strategies (CANVAS) is run by Slobodan Djinovic and Srdja Popovic. It operates a network of international trainers and consultants with experience in successful democratic movements. Visit the website at https://canvasopedia.org.

2 Srdja Popovic et al., "A Guide to Effective Nonviolent Struggle," CANVAS Core Curriculum (2007), https://canvasopedia.org/project/canvas-core-curriculum/.

3 Our team of researchers included Madison Ambrose, Katrina Burka, Suzanna Maize, Julio Pardo, and Channalyn Tek.

4 Ronald Reagan, "Inaugural Address" (California Gubernatorial Inauguration, January 5, 1967), https://www.reaganlibrary.gov/research/speeches/01051967a.

5 Erica Chenoweth and Maria J. Stephan, *Why Civil Resistance Works: The Strategic Logic of Nonviolent Conflict* (New York: Columbia University Press, 2011).

6 David Robson, "The '3.5% rule': How a Small Minority Can Change the World," *BBC News* (May 13, 2019), https://www.bbc.com/future/article/20190513-it-only-takes-35-of-people-to-change-the-world.

7 Popovic, "Guide to Effective Nonviolent Struggle."

8 The Yes Men is a group that has worked "with activist orgs and university groups. Before that, we were more like lone vigilantes." Learn more about them on their website, http://theyesmen.org.

9 Stephen Holden, "All Suited Up for Mischief, to Rumple Stuffed Shirts," *New York Times,* October 6, 2009, https://www.nytimes.com/2009/10/07/movies/07yes.html.

10 For a more detailed account of this, see my book: Srdja Popovic, *Blueprint for Revolution* (New York: Spiegel & Grau, 2015), 37–40.

11 "Myanmar Parties in Dispute over Bamboo Hat," *Reuter,* July 2, 2010, https://www.reuters.com/article/oukoe-uk-myanmar-politics-hat-idUKTRE6611DC20100702.

12 Véronique Dudouet, "Nonviolent Resistance in Power Asymmetries," in *Advancing Conflict Transformation: The Berghof Handbook II*, ed. Beatrix Austin, Martina Fischer, and Hans J. Giessmann (Opladen: Barbara Budrich, 2011), https://www.berghof-foundation.org/fileadmin/redaktion/Publications/Handbook/Articles/dudouet_handbookII.pdf.

13 Tara John. "Evan Mawarire, Pastor behind Zimbabwe's #ThisFlag Protest Movement, Denied Bail," *Time,* February 4, 2017, https://time.com/4659284/evan-mawarie-zimbabwe-this-flag-bail-denied.

14 Cristina Rodriguez et al, "Holograms for Freedom," *Docubase* (MIT, 2015), https://docubase.mit.edu/project/holograms-for-freedom.

15 Majken Jul Sørensen and Brian Martin, "Dilemma Actions" (June 17, 2014), 129. https://www.wri-irg.org/sites/default/files/public_files/12%20Dilemma%20actions.pdf.

16 Andrew Boyd and Joshua Kahn Russell, "Put Your Target in a Decision Dilemma," *Beautiful Trouble: A Toolbox for Revolution* (New York: OR Books, 2012), 166–67, https://beautifultrouble.org/principle/put-your-target-in-a-decision-dilemma.

17 The Global Nonviolent Action Database is available at https://nvdatabase.swarthmore.edu.

18 Sophia A. McClennen and Remy M. Maisel, *Is Satire Saving Our Nation? Mockery and American Politics* (New York: Palgrave Macmillan, 2016). This source offers more evidence on the positive effects of satirical protest for democracy.

19 Majken Jul Sørensen, *Humour in Political Activism: Creative Nonviolent Resistance* (New York: Palgrave Macmillan, 2016). Also see her dissertation, "Humorous Political Stunts: Nonviolent Public Challenges to Power," PhD diss., School of Humanities and Social Inquiry, University of Wollongong, 2014, https://ro.uow.edu.au/theses/4291.

20 Sarah Freeman-Woolpert. "Why Nazis Are So Afraid of These Clowns," *Waging Nonviolence,* February 22, 2019, https://wagingnonviolence.org/2017/08/nazis-afraid-clowns/?pf=true.

21 "Finnish Clowns Mock Anti-Immigrant Patrols by Surrounding Them in Song," *CBC News,* January 21, 2016, https://www.cbc.ca/news/trending/loldiers-of-odin-finland-1.3410837.

22 Kevin O'Flynn, "Toys Cannot Hold Protest Because They Are Not Citizens of Russia, Officials Rule," *Guardian,* February 15, 2012, https://www.theguardian.com/world/2012/feb/15/toys-protest-not-citizens-russia.

23 Anne Wyman, "Burmese Women Campaign for Human Rights (Panties for Peace), 2007," *Global Nonviolent Action*

Database (Swarthmore College, February 27, 2012), https://nvdatabase.swarthmore.edu/content/burmese-women-campaign-human-rights-panties-peace-2007.

24 Sophia A. McClennen, "The Bitter Irony of Donald Trump," *Salon,* December 22, 2017, https://www.salon.com/2017/12/23/the-bitter-irony-of-donald-trump.

25 Srdja Popovic and Mladen Joksic, "Why Dictators Don't Like Jokes," *Foreign Policy,* April 5, 2013, https://foreignpolicy.com/2013/04/05/why-dictators-dont-like-jokes. Also see McClennen and Maisel, *Is Satire Saving Our Nation?*

26 Jody C. Baumgartner, Amy B. Becker, and Sophia A. McClennen, "The Joke Is on You: Satire and Blowback," *Political Humor in a Changing Media Landscape: A New Generation of Research,* ed. Jody C Baumgartner and Amy B. Becker (Lanham: Lexington Books, 2018), 137–56. This provides more on the blowback to satirical actions.

27 George Lakey, *Powerful Peacemaking: A Strategy for a Living Revolution* (Philadelphia: New Society Publishers, 1987).

28 Philippe Duhamel, "The Dilemma Demonstration: Using Nonviolent Civil Disobedience to Put the Government between a Rock and a Hard Place," *A Tactical Notebook*, ed. Nancy L. Pearson (St. Paul, Minn.: Center for Victims of Torture, 2004), https://www.academia.edu/7263696/Dilemma_Demonstration_P_Duhamel_v2.

29 The question "Did it attract media attention?" could be construed as a sort of selection bias because if the dilemma action did not gain media attention, the case would not be known (therefore the success percentage for this question is understandably high).

30 Due to the categorical nature of binary statistics, the question "Did the dilemma action reduce the risk of severe punishment to

activists, or in cases of an oppressive response by authority, make the punishment backfire?" is particularly skewed to configure an exact answer, as the outcome varies in nature. Still, we measured this by determining the severity of the punishment. If that was still N/A, we looked at whether the oppressive answer to the activists backfired.

31 For these data, see Erica Chenoweth and Christopher Wiley Shay, "List of Campaigns in NAVCO 1.3" (Harvard Dataverse, 2020), https://doi.org/10.7910/DVN/ON9XND.

32 If you want more examples of dilemma actions, you can also look at the Global Nonviolent Action Database (https://nvdatabase. swarthmore.edu), which offers free access to hundreds of completed examples of nonviolent action. All of this work by activists offers inspiration for your nonviolent actions for democracy. We may emphasize slightly different tactics, but all theories of dilemma actions have a common thread: force the government to be stuck in a dilemma where if they do nothing to stop the protesters, they look bad, and if they intervene, they look even worse.

33 Christopher Brandt et al., "Freedom in the World 2019" (Freedom House, 2019), https://freedomhouse.org/sites/default/files/Feb2019_FH_FITW_2019_Report_ForWeb-compressed.pdf.

About the Authors

Srdja Popovic is executive director of the Centre for Applied Nonviolent Action and Strategies (CANVAS) and author of several books on nonviolent movements, including *Blueprint For Revolution: How to Use Rice Pudding, Lego Men, and Other Nonviolent Techniques to Galvanize Communities, Overthrow Dictators, or Simply Change the World.* He is also a cofounder of the Center for Civic Resilience and 53rd rector of St. Andrews University in Scotland.

Sophia A. McClennen is professor of international affairs and comparative literature at Penn State University and founding director of the Center for Global Studies. She has published eleven books including *Is Satire Saving Our Nation?* and *The Routledge Companion to Literature and Human Rights.*

Milton Keynes UK
Ingram Content Group UK Ltd.
UKHW011900070324
439052UK00004B/261